Adventures of the
TORTOISESHELL CAT

June Weaver Martin

LifeRich Publishing is a registered trademark of The Reader's Digest Association, Inc.

LifeRich Publishing books may be ordered through booksellers or by contacting:

LifeRich Publishing
1663 Liberty Drive
Bloomington, IN 47403
www.liferichpublishing.com
1 (888) 238-8637

Because of the dynamic nature of the Internet, any web addresses or links contained in this book may have changed since publication and may no longer be valid. The views expressed in this work are solely those of the author and do not necessarily reflect the views of the publisher, and the publisher hereby disclaims any responsibility for them.

Any people depicted in stock imagery provided by Thinkstock are models, and such images are being used for illustrative purposes only.
Certain stock imagery © Thinkstock.

ISBN: 978-1-4897-1221-9 (sc)
ISBN: 978-1-4897-1220-2 (e)

Print information available on the last page.

LifeRich Publishing rev. date: 03/17/2017

Our family had seen the colorful cat several times around our neighborhood and in the wooded area near our home. She was always very shy and skittish.

Her hair was all different colors, black, gray, orange and yellow with white feet. We said that she was "so ugly that she was pretty!" She seemed to be a stray cat looking for food for her family.

Early one morning we saw her in our driveway nursing her newborn kittens. When we tried to go near her, she immediately ran and started taking the kittens away. After that experience, we did not see her for a long time, until the day that she again appeared at our house.

The Mother cat appeared to be very smart, but shy and timid. We began to feed them and play with them when they came by. They began to like being at our house. It was very evident that the Mother cat and the kittens had been mistreated, being chased away from other people's houses, and having very little food to eat.

One day, a friend came by to visit me. She saw the cat and said, "Oh, you have a tortoise-shell cat! I had never heard of this kind of a cat-- a tortoise-shell cat.

Later, I went to the local library and found a book about tortoise-shell cats. The book said that tortoise-shell cats are usually female. They are very intelligent and like attention, but sometimes, all of a sudden, will bite or scratch someone who may be very good to her or might be playing with her or her little kittens.

As time went on, the cat continued to stay around our house most of the time. She had more kittens out in the woods or at our house. She seemed very content to stay at our house.

It was evident that the Mama cat liked our family more and more and was very comfortable there. She also had a mind of her own and wanted to make her own decisions. She was very intelligent.

After a while, she had another litter of four kittens. One morning we found her and her kittens in a basket in a remote spot of the carport of the house where we live.

Our family was so excited about the cat having kittens again. I picked up one of the kittens to look at it. The Mama cat did not want her kittens to be picked up by anyone!

The next morning the Mama cat and the little ones were gone! We looked everywhere, but could not find them anywhere! One day, she brought them back to the house and put them near a corner of the house in a bunch of leaves.

A few days later, it looked as though it would rain and the little kittens would get wet. So the Mama cat began moving them again. I happened to find her in the process of moving them. She put a frown on her face almost like a person. She was so intelligent–almost like a human!

My husband, Mr. Bob, really did not like cats very much. At that time, however, he took a liking to the tortoise-shell cat and started feeding her every day.

The book mentioned earlier stated that the tortoise-shell cats would bite or scratch a person without any reason. Well, that is what happened one day when Mr. Bob was feeding her.

The cat jumped up and bit him on his arm. This made Mr. Bob very angry!

Mr. Bob kicked the cat as hard as he could across the yard and refused to ever have anything else to do with her.

Well, the cat learned her lesson. We never heard of her biting anyone else except for a couple of times.

One day, I was playing with one of her kittens when she put her mouth on my hand as though to bite, but did not hurt me. I did feel the teeth, but no pain..

She seemed to think, all of a sudden, that she should not bite! I have never heard except for a couple of times that she has tried to bite someone again!

After giving away all of the kittens, we now have only the tortoise-shell cat and her adult female child. They feel very close to each other and are often seen around the house lying or sitting very close to each other.

They seem to love each other very much and have a mother-daughter or a sisterly love together. The daughter cat did give birth to five kittens not long ago.

When the kittens got too big to stay on the carport for fear of getting hurt, we put them on a screened-in porch. When the mother cat (the tortoise-shell cat) could get into the screened-in porch area, she would lie down and nurse the kittens.

Also, when the kittens were first born, she was constantly taking the kittens out of the box they were in and trying to take them some other place! She wanted to be in control!

However, we did not let her get on the porch very often. She would then sit around all the time staring longingly at the little kittens!

Being almost human, it was obvious that she was very envious and jealous and badly wanted to be in there where all the action was. We did not allow it, however.

We soon found a home for all five of the little kittens and now have only the two adult cats at home which seem to be enough for us at the present time. The two seem to get along fine!